AF689895

"If any individual lives too much in relations, so that (s)he becomes a stranger to the resources of his (her) own nature, (s)he falls, after a while, into a distraction or imbecility which can only be cured by a time of isolation which gives the renovating fountains time to rise up."

Margaret Fuller— "Women In The Nineteenth Century"

Hysterical Fugue

Susan Lawton

The term "Hysterical Fugue" was coined during the turn of the century to describe the condition of ladies who frequently vanished, then returned several days later claiming amnesia. The most famous case is that of Agatha Christie, but her's is just one of many. Women have always employed methods of escape, be it madness, illness, amnesia or more positively, writing.

hys-ter-i-cal (hi ster i kel) adj. uncontrollably emotional
(Greek: 'of the womb')

fugue (fyoog) Psychiatry. a period during which a patient suffers from a loss of memory, often begins a new life, and upon recovery, remembers nothing of the amnesic period.
(Latin: 'flight')

© Copyright 1982 by Susan Lawton

ISBN: 0-937998-07-9
ISSN: 0195-7848

Number 80 of a limited edition of 500 books.

Photographs by Lee Kuebler—St. Thomas, U.S.V.I.

Cumberland Journal
P.O. Box 2648
Harrisburg, PA 17105

For my Mother, who finally taught me that all things are possible.

Hysterical Fugue

Hystericál Fugue

Pulled up from sleep by some soft row,
the sand, confused, refuses eyes.
Startled, I peel off the warmth
of eiderdown, prepare to leave
the goldened room.

Pad to the door like a timid tiger,
and the darkness melts in
as goldness melts out, leaving
a pattern of arched light
in the freshly fallen snow.

Mystified by moment and purity of light.
A glance at the silent films
of consciousness.

Weightless and filigree, the curtains
hang, and each detail observed,
and reckoned with
like Flemish dewdrops on a perfect rose
(the firelight ignites the voiceless walls)

Winds nip at the long black dress
as I skim the perimeters of grace
peering into this indefinable house.

Intricate hands finger the hems.
I hide the child in soft pleats,
turn back towards the sea, and walk.
Carrying dawn in my womb,
affirmed to return
and to speak of it.

Aegeaniana

In Bodrum where the night falls fast
and dawning gently climbs the lazy hills
where olive trees and wild goats
prepare to soak the Turkish sun
I met myself.

In Ephesus, my name was carved
in marbled streets where sea jewels
used to reach. My ancientness
heard old voices from the ampitheatre
knew masks of forgotten kings
and innocents.

For a stone, I'd go back there
to harder home
seek the blue eyed owl in Athena's house
dye my hands orange and prepare to wed
the earth
swim crystal waters above Hellenistic shards
and sea spines with poison for my veins.

I am the child of many countries
but first birth came in dark nights
from the faceless mother
of Aegean stones.

Turkish Woman

Ten miles outside of Istanbul, you can still
buy a wife for a goat and a few sacks of grain.

She is thick, wrapped black
carries the water jug
following steep paths
placing each footfall
as if it mattered
to the lessons of earth.

Her neck strains high
and shoulders trace
the motions of passing
rocks.

How poised, seems proud
gold tooth catching sun
reflects the light
of labors, never ending

And if she were
to spill one drop
from the cistern
of her fears
would armies rise up
or tiger lilies bloom?

Botany

for Pamela

It took most of spring
to show you magnolia
from dogwood.
Magnolia blushed pink
like lotus, I said
dogwood petals spread wide.

Now chestnuts bloom before us
large   white   cones
will turn to hard shells in fall
but we have summer yet before us.

Forsythia gone
and you have loved them
better than I
Encouraged saffron blossoms
to brighten your room
long before their appointed time

as aster pods turn silently
in the night-soil
we turn slowly
in our separate dreams.

This has taken years!
Where was it that botany began?
From flower, stalk, to root . . .

Spring has warmed us
caused green shoots
to bind us close
your lily of the valley
come to sweeten the day
of my grass harp.

Small Dark Women

He had this strange affinity
for small dark women
banking that they
might read his mind
like tea leaves

crawl into the soft curve
of his yang

take shorthand and all the rest.

How tall I stand
beside him
snaking the words
'round his pride
to please him
reading his palms
choosing his ties

pretending affinity
for small dark men
while searching
for the white underbelly
on which to pin him.

From Nine To Five

Every morning
along with tea and toast
I shoot up ink
into the main artery.

It is a necessary evil.
It is expected
if you dare to expect
to maintain your place
in this game.

It eventually turns black
your heart

and gives you

the distinct opportunity
to toss the dice
one
more
time.

Gestalt This Dream

I am the dark haired woman.
I am the blonde one too.
I am also the blonde one's child.
The child which vanishes into air.

I am the beast which carries
these women
up the leaf strewn hill.
I am the hill.
I am the leaves.

I am the vanished child
calling in the distance.
I am the monolith of letterpress type
beautiful, with Gothic O's and P's
I am each letter.

I am the blonde one who will not yield
to the death which the dark one deals.

I am the beetle which the blonde one becomes
trapped, in the monolith of type.

I am the warm rain.
I am the the startled lovers
who can not bear
the sight
of me.

Meditations On The Tomb Of Tutankhamen

The study of surface
when words probe too deep
probe silent places
cave quiet, no breathing
no rustling of grasses
and we can hardly believe in sun
or rain
just the consistency of blackness
the little hairs which tickle
our lips
our eyes
make jest of living things
things with eyes
with claws.
There are no more dawns
no romance of moon
on arms
on breasts.
Only grains of wheat
can hold these secrets.
Gold, the tales of art, of beauty
but grain   holds fast   the life.

Ode To Bread

O, bread
you have given yourself to me again.
In this small space you have doubled
been beaten down, and have doubled again
for me.

Your yeast has devoured my honey treats
and I know how proud you are to rise

and you have history, my bread
raised or flattened
Gentile and Jew have been nurtured by you

my bread

and I will savour you like manna
flesh of my flesh
I will worship you as wine.

Dangerous Things

The night when the moon was covered with lichen
and the branches cried like tiny souls falling
from their beds to crush their tiny skulls

Ah, you say the showers will make our roses bloom,
Too much, I say, and the tomatoes will rot

Together in this world we go on inventing tales
to keep one another from sleep
Embellish childish wounds to feel the knives cut,
car doors slam on our long white fingers, note
the entry points of broken glass and count the
stitches which left behind their marks

Tell me again about your cousin
who lost his head in the harvester
about the cat with no front paws. . .
The child who drown in flax seeds.

Wind splits the night and is a masochistic stranger.
Knows no bounds

Tell me again about the man with no head
Did the head cry out?
Did the body try to run away?

You leave to watch the lightning
I refuse to leave this bed
ever again.

Facing Eviction

There is no safety
for you for I
to leave this house
alone
unarmed.

We know too much
about one another.

I clammer down the stairs
bare and wooden
for the third time
you need only hear the sound
prepare the ice

you come home from the world
back curved
I get the bourbon
close the books
remove your boots

it is in this house
this crooked walled
and windy place
where it sometimes rains
above the bed

we have slowly come
to know
which plants will grow
in the darkest corners
that roaches do not conspire
to steal our children
from their beds

the only safe place is here
where you hold my hand in sleep
where we whisper fears
that no one hears.

Monday's Argument

like butter

it arcs
across
the table

slides from
our tongues
& lands.

the pat
perpendicular
to the floor

for
just
one
moment . . .

before

it melts
into our
oriental
carpet.

What Is Missing Here

These still mornings
leftovers of the dead night air
mornings when the dew never dries
both towels smell of mold by 4 pm
and all we want is wind
cool and from the north
slow wind to finger the leaves
as if they were Alençon lace.

These still mornings
in a solid block of weeks.

This one is different
missing your chest
almost too warm to touch
fingering your soft down
with painted nails to awaken you
licking your eyelids like a mother cat.

That is what is missing here
wishing you here

come back to me whole,
come back to me,
to me,
come,

I will clean the air for you
draw a wind from azure blue and swan's down
wash the towels in Perrier
rose petals for this bed

come back to me, whole,
come back to me
come to me
whole.

Poem Pertaining To Suffocation

As you sit on me
Hold my hands high
above my head
Blow kisses to my eyes

I conjure you beast
great cat
readying yourself
to suck the life
from my milky breath.

Playing Dictionary

In the dictionary
the word onerous
comes before . . . oneself
meaning
the obligations
outweigh advantages,
and oneself, sane condition
"to feel like one's own self"

The word which follows these
is one-shot, and this
means, only once.

I leave you now,
the obligation to myself
out weigh my ties with you
and I do not believe in
one-shot deals, or one time
loves, or one-track minds

and further on, consider
the onion of the lily
family, having
multi-layers, with
a thin but strong
translucent skin.

The Light Change & Unlearning

Mornings, the sun so strong
  upon the waters
that I can not each my peach
  or drink my jasmine tea
upon the porch

by midday, the profusion
  of our plants
will hide from directed sun
  instead soak rays
from the stillness of air

I can sit, feet up
  in the $6.99 beach chairs
lick the gooey green of avocado
  from its skin
watch the cats play in tall grasses

    begin to try unlearning

at 4, Annie comes around
  with cold beer and cheeses
we sit like that, talking low
  laughing loud like mallards
waiting for sunset

    i only notice the shadows
    erasing each detail of the leaves

Mosquitos join us, so we dine inside
  the high ceiling reminds us
of Casablanca or Tiepolo
  the white, she recalls a country church
and I, my own lost self

    i have come here to unlearn you

She leaves, and I put on Gershwin
  wrapped up in blues
I begin to get a little low
  listening to the borrowed fridge
humming all things cold

I try to shake you out
  by writing you
but you stick like a burr
  and sometimes my womb aches
as if it were still called home

I pull myself up each steep step
  to the cathedral place
where the bed stands firmly
  centered between the magnetic
orange and blue

i have come here to unlearn you, by
  learning me. Only then can i understand
which of your pains was real

The darkness sails through small windows
  cats have cuddled so close
that I dare not move a muscle
  and I will dream again that
the child was yours

I will dream again that it is living
  with a born again family
in Wisconson, and that its hair is
  the color of wheat
but I can not decipher her name

i have come here to unlearn you, to
  find out which of my pains
was real. This may take a long time

In Absentia

Innocent of all life.
Nebulous as milkweed.

Apostate I have born
bittersweet bonds of love
silhouetted in blood
endearing you to me
never mentioning you
that brought me close to death.
In this garden, my child
asters whisper you name.

Edwin & the Pianos

Edwin knew where all the pianos were.
He had maps of the city,
marked the buildings containing the pianos
with different colored pins.
Blue was for Baldwin.

You would think that Edwin
loved to play
but he didn't.
He just liked to know
in case somebody asked him.

Sometimes I've heard Gershwin
from the apartment next door.
That's where Edwin lives.
He claims it's a recording
but I've seen his fingerprints
on the keys.
I know that they are his
as I've tested them with talcum powder
and they match the ones on the sherry glasses
that he always leaves in my sink.

He will not let me take his photograph
he says he is unphotogenic
I am afraid that he is invisible
like Gershwin.

You might think that I am in love with Edwin,
but you are wrong.
I just like to know where he is
in case I need him.

I might be all wrong about Edwin
but I know that I am right about one thing.
Blue is for Baldwin.

The Magician

It appears you have a deep concern
that my love poems to you have stopped.
You admit to feeling like the silk stockings
(usually employed to strap you to chairs)
are being dragged across your face.
You are alone at night in your rainbow sheets
counting the times we've made love,
needing both hands, but only one time.
Watching the silks mute your visions
catching softness as it crosses
your lips—the faint scent of Aliage
still clinging to the points which would
fall at the backs of the knees.

I have been witness to you.
How you stuff 20 colored scarves
into your tight little fists
and ending up with only air
to show for it.
Capturing coins from behind my ears
you once conjured me heiress,
thought me worthy of your throne.

What you've revealed, you now
carefully conceal.
We pretend like none of this matters
any more than the rich sweet moment
of the first summer strawberry.

Oh, lavender you, in the quiet section
of the night
I hum your name in French
Alter the distortions to fit into the moments
as if for the love
and the getting of it,
as if, for the love, and the giving of it . . .

I have pulled 20 colored scarves
from beneath my pillow, tied them together
bound my hands and my feet
and swaddled myself in prisms.

I am pointing myself towards the moon
like an arrow from your long bow
I escape,
leaving you with only
a grazed arm.

Focal Point

As you have told me before,
it is all a matter of focus.

When muscles draw the lenses
to just the right shape
I will see you
for what you really are.

In the soft nights
when the wine stains
the sheets
and July breezes
breathe on your strong
sweet flesh . . .

I can remember you
when you were nearer
than now

Your face was softer,
and love stronger
from the unknowing
of it

I gather these halos
embellish you as
what I thought
was Michael
when you were rowing
me closer to the shore.

Blake Leaving Paris

It was no use trying to get him out. He had brought it upon himself after all. Four nights in a row we all heard him banging on the door, screaming "Holy Christ, someone let me in!" We'd all had keys made for him on various occasions, but keys were unimportant to Blake. The sewers of Paris will probably back up some day from a dam built of Blake's keys.

The concierge had had it up to here tonight. Being half black, she hid her café au lait flesh and let his voice pierce through the shuttered windows.

The police came tonight and took Blake away. Eight of them in capes and hats and no guns. They put Blake into a wagon, screaming, and took him away to god knows where. The concierge said that he was crazy, that he was trying to break in, that she had never seen him before. We watched, helplessly, from the appropriately French windows, resting breasts on the wrought iron railing, the night still holding eyelids half shut.

Blake returned on Wednesday, at around noon, to collect his twenty odd notebooks, volumes of Tolstoy, and posters of Lenin. He was sober this time when he broke into my room asking for a cup of my Earl Grey tea and leaving, as usual, with 20 francs. We discussed the possibilities of making love, but he decided that it might fatigue his intellectual energies. It was never any good anyway. Just warmed the bed a little.

Blake was the only person I'd ever known who lived on his intellectual energies. He was never happy, but I often wonder if he was winning.

I watched him disappear down Rue Henri-Barbusse, slouching, his dark hair scattered around his pale face. All poets are pale. It is a requirement, even for crazy Russian ones. It had never occurred to me before why he chose the name Blake, why he chose to break down my door looking for tea, or if it was true that his parents were killed on the steps like in an Eisenstein film.

It didn't really matter. He was crazy and forgot my keys.

The French Sailors

— Bermuda, Oct. '81

One dark, the other one fair,
spit brass and sighing lights
they have come here
to wrap their clean, white arms
around our cotillion waists,
to take gravity from our tiny bones
that we may be earth bound
only by their long strips
of love.

Breathing a few
well chosen phrases
into our shell-like ears
expecting rushing of oceans
storms of bees
singing in the frangipani trees.
Expecting to twist our souls
& screw them into passing stallions
of white clouds. . .

We courtsey,
inquire for their children,
their wives,
and close the lights.

Father Poem: Number 27

I am not done yet.
I need to tell you
of the last time
                    we made time
    to
    touch.

It was in New York City
    it was snowing.
We ate lamb chops
    drank good German wine.

I gave him my poems.
We dipped fresh strawberries
    into
the white porcelain sugar bowl
    we talked of France
my living there
                    his never coming.

He walked 3 blocks
                    walked me to the train . . .
We stopped 3 times
                    for him to catch his breath . . .
He
  made me promise
                        not to tell.

I called his wife that night
                        to tell.

The next time I saw him
                        he was ashes
in a plain   brown   wrapper.

We had eaten fresh strawberries together
                    in the middle of December
We had dipped them into our wine
                    then into the sugar
                    to coat them in sweetness
no one said goodbye

Orphaned (a recurring dream)

it takes
almost
3
years
after Daddy's
death
(as if he did
possess that death)
twenty years
after the time
he
waited for me
standing
on that rock
outside of Brookdale School
waited there
to take me home with him.

Living With The Legends

Daddy, I've brought into
all your legends.
What do I do now
with all your "joie de vivre"
with all this sensitivity
that creeps into the seams
of our borrowing
one anothers dreams?

"Touch the stars," you told me
so I do.
"Now touch this earth,"
and now I can.
But where have you gone
in the midst of all this?
I waken every morning
and feel your sun
warm all things green,
turn my white sheets
pink, like pure Bermuda sand. . .

Why are you sleeping
as if nothing were happening?

Only the sun is real
and the moon is sometimes
full
All the rest is fantasy.

Touch me from where you are now
beyond all of this
come touch me and tell me
that it will never be cold.

I am so much of you
like you're the core of me
and what I want is nothing less
than everything
that childhood promised
and more.

Legends come cheap
but loneliness can last
a whole lifetime, if you let it
and I do.

Conditions

You will have little
Or no use for me.
Childless, without a bone
for soup.

Asked if you'd love me
if I lost all my teeth,
your answer   no

Dreams get beached
like the great whales
they suffocate
with the air
and rot in the morning sun.

One time when very poor
mother made soup
from fish heads,
soft onions
and a sprig of thyme.

it fed father for 3 nights

he unplaited her thick
brown hair
and took her to bed.

The Trade

My mother's dreams
were warm and full
of me.

The apple was I
full and round.

Surprise for her
40th birthday.

The task at hand
and a handful
was I.

Walked at 7 months
and ran soon after

Challenge the apron strings
to bind my tiny wrists

They never did
until now

I feel my heart stop
Mother

With each and every
tumble that you
take.

Like Alice, You Caruso

When life seemed kinder to us
when the moon seemed captured
in the Waterford crystal
and the grass was as soft
as the down of your chest

The elements conspired with us
the night erasing our words
the wind carrying off
rich scents of our love

These were the times
you ignited the night
kept the chill well beyond
any space in which you held me

This aching is a pearl
growing larger with each day

I would come to you again
sporting cold beajolais
if only I could rub your shoulders
call out the genie
the one who made you larger
than your life

But like Alice, I stepped back
through the mirror
and you, still like Caruso
wandering the nights alone?

This nostalgia feels deadly
does little to warm the frosting
from the panes, yet carries me
somehow closer to
your skin

Tomorrow, for just one moment
come to me as in a dream
ignite the lamps

I will wait, not daring to question the wind.

What Happened In Leaving

for Madeline Tiger Bass

After leaving you
cradled in that huge yellow cab,
I got swallowed up in black
in dark
stuffed to the gills
and almost breathless
carrying your poems
wondering who will give the funds
to make tiny paper boats
out of your babies
to sail as far as Ibiza, St. Tropez
perhaps beyond.

After leaving lovers,
mostly the men
with ebony eyes
there is little left
those sorrows and
"should have saids"

but here, but now
there is even blood
deep wound on my left hand
the fleshy part
leaving stains on London Fog
a place which you have loved
as if virginity was lost
to some Muse
as if there were answers
inscribed
in flesh.

A Short Apology To Judith Whose Book I Printed Drunk

After 3 bourbons with Marian
(who must know more than God himself)
understanding all my double entendre
and wet eyed tales about my mother

I come back here, to the past
pitch black,
light headed and high
above these inks.
Something intrinsic takes over
knows which knobs to push and
to pull, to start
and to stop.

Printing feels primal,
like sucking
as the ink transfers
like it should
from roller to blanket
to poems. . .

We sat in our bar
munching crackers
full of cheddar cheese
Somewhere our ink
transfering from
roller to blanket
to love
and now I feel closer
than this old "om"
that the press makes
driving my blood home.

We've know this before,
counted rosaries
in our sleep, and lovers
in the same breath.
We've shared more than
blisters and colds
with these rembrandt brown,
regal blues and jet blacks
our fathers died,
mothers went mad
yet we've carried our names
as if they were "Job"

Pressing these sheets
between blanket and chrome
making words for the others
who pay
like we've paid for our losses
triumphed our gains
and after all of the pain
for ever remains
this peace.

transfering from blanket to poem

I am not counting the sheets
as I should
rather transfering from pencil
to poem
how each day that you've stood
here beside me
has entered deep,
leaving me whole.

Free Admission, Name Dropping, Love, Lust, Incest & Cultism Within the Ranks of Small Pressers

I admit to being the woman
in the arms of Eric Brazier
outside the Riverview Motel
in Harrisburg, PA.

I have also spent several consecutive months
in love with Geo. Myers Jr.
It was just incestuous lust
He looks like my brother.
Enclosed is a photo of me
in case you want to compare.

He married someone else.
I went to Harrisburg to watch.
We write occasionally.
Rarely to each other.
We never drank together.

I have had dinner with Richard Grayson
three times.
He is glad that I don't jog.
This is a secret.
I bought 3 of his books.
This is not a secret.
He makes me laugh.
He doesn't drink.

We talk about George sometimes.
We both love him secretly, I think.
He didn't marry either one of us.

I have gotten drunk with Kevin Urick.
He wore my hat
had holes in his shoes.
I wrote a poem about him,
but he rejected it.
Enclosed please find said poem
for your consideration.

I once printed a poster for Lawrence Ferlinghetti.
I have written 5 poems to him.
He has written several times.
I have never met him.
I have remained faithful to him.

Rick Peabody would not dance with me
at George's wedding.
He talked all night about Tatum O'Neal.
He took the photograph at the Riverview Motel.

I admit to secret thrills about my review
in "The Smudge".
Enclosed, please find $20.00.
Send 2 more of this issue, resubscribe me,
use the rest for cold beer.
If you are ever in New York, look me up.
I never tell anyone any secrets.

About the Author

for George Myers, Jr.

"Explorer" my ass!
Like that last time in Istanbul
when you went hunting for
the speck of red pepper
between the incisor and bicuspid.
It was almost embarrassing
with you in there like that
right in front of the Spice Bazaar.
I tried to talk you into a chunk
of Halvah instead
but you were put off by the flies
and dirty footed six year olds
selling river water.

And about that "Botanist" stuff,
at Ephesus you couldn't distinguish
oregano from lambs ears.
Thought basil to be thyme.

"Inventor" yes, I'll buy that one
for your stories wove a web of magic
in those soft nights
when the stars and planets knew our names
and theirs were Zeus's children.

About that "Swordsman" part
I've nothing more to say
except that death never came swift,
seldom inhabited stones or fruit . . .

"Editor, Publisher" . . . did you edit
those words you unfurled into my ear
or did they spill like mead from nectar flowers
as I first supposed, and speaking of suppose
have those gems been read by others in your poems?

Writing all of this leaves me somewhat cold,
terribly tired and bitchy
for no more soft nights bind us to ourselves.
The space for greeting is as small as the eye
of a serpent's child and in this shadow shape
that smells like juniper in sleep
I conform your fiction to fit me
like those leather thongs which once protected
my feet.

Harrisburg Poem

Silence, so heavy
it pushes on the eardrums
makes sounds   hums
higher than a hummingbird's.

Everyone has gone, sped off
high hum   tires on wet pavement
traveling 3 hours to Washington
eating rabbit paté
in a beaujolais fog.

Thighs hummed
as I phoned up Grayson
                    who sings
measel blues and reds
my bankamericard ticking away
                         the seconds
like cicadas songs,

I didn't care

until the rug started to foam
t.v. screamed   hard,
disrupting the hums

and the best man never arrived
to carry me gently.

Fish & Fowl

In the picture frame setting
of the arched doorway,
I watched from the galley,
far back as I could,
how a naked man took a knife
to a dolphin fish.

I saw no details,
not the blood or the white flesh
ripped from the glittering
rainbow of skin.
Saw only the rhythms of the man
as the knife cut loose a life.

I have told Michael
while he readied himself
to kill ducks
"The only life we have
the right to take
is our own."

These men things won't hear me.
It is hard to swallow the spoils
of their insults
no matter what the sauce.

For Jack Who Came To See Me But Never Made It Past The Bronx

Hooked up again
like some old trout
you seem kinder
to them
than to me
you travel farther
cross the woods
in rain
but dare not brave
the Bronx for me.

My dear brother
bearer of the name
keeper of the keys
you flash them
in front of my smiles
replace them quickly
in the pocket
of your old jeans
before I have had time
to count them
feel them
taste them like
a blind child might.

They would be bitter
to the tongue.

We are bound by flesh
you and I
my blood
my only one
like siamese twins
joined at the spine
we share one heart
often hold hands
but can not taste
the other's tears.

Untitled

Swallowing the root in silence.
Keeping the darkness in.
Holding on to the moisture,
as if the leeching of it
would dry our very bones.

In silence, swallowing the root
of all this pain.
Gagging on dis-communication.
Praying for the patience
feeling the soft flesh of the heart
turn stone.

Lying Pillows

I want a pillow printed all over with
HARD, HARD, HARD, HARD
preferably from Bloomingdale's
just like the ones here
that whisper
soft, soft, soft, soft.
I enjoy the truth, however twisted.

On The Russian River

On the Russian River, maybe
six or seven years gone by
inhabited by the sons of salesmen
daughters of the eastern elite
I knew a man called Richard there
fine gentle eyes and foreign colors
gathered in his hands
to send one to the sky,
torment the hours with other lives
past incarnations,
Mad like Zelda, Anne or Sylvia
never Virginia Woolf
not ½ as bright
but stars shone hard on that river
and the water offered carriage home
but I declined, prefering absinthe
to acid, sorrow to stones.
I never met a man with eyes like that
for men had no names
kept separate by their fingers.
How many left beside the grand hotel?
Listen hard for my spirit
for I found there, and lost
that slender reed whose tune
I knew by heart
but never sang in unison.

Mount St. Helens

We stood very still
Grey ash
first, a light frosting
took the highlights
from our hair.

Soon
our toes disappeared.

We didn't move
one
muscle.

It took, perhaps
just moments
before our lungs
grew grey,
trees began
their moaning.
We were
more stoic
than the trees.

Seeking Pompeii
our last touch
of immortality.

After the Falling

It is a hardened place
where the stones have withered
in their beds
& flowers are just memories
of lusher times.

Times when I could come to know
the coldness of a cascade stream
in spring
belong to it
like the hermit crab
belongs to his stolen home.

Remember when food fell to us
Landed in my calico lap.
The cherries, apples and golden pears
ripe beyond our believing.

You taught me how to suck nectar
from the honeysuckle flower
avoid spiders amid the blackberry vines

Now days form a grey mist
from the essential motion
of dawning and
I have changed from new,
to borrowing this,
a sad and sorrowed skin.

We will lose our souls
when the mountain comes to anger.
You told me this.

I sift thru the ash
looking for your one
true possession

& consider you Alladin
asking for the wrong wish.

Palmprints (identifying life)

It was something about a secret, I think . . .
Each word
like the poems
well chosen
savoured
and unexplained

Interpretation to be made by reader . . . .
then forgotten
like the dusk
as it calls the island names
like "black"
like "warm"
as if the night began and ended
here

it is true, I believe . . .
for I have the palmprints
to prove it.

the clues to this are few
kept hidden within the walls
fingered only by
the creatures which are passing

the promise
that down the road
there will be fewer rocks
more stones still sunwarm
and sorrows find their homes
in blades of grass.

Mythology

Madness!
That across this oaken table
I can not see
my own reflection
in your clear glass eye.

I will come to you again
straddling the seams of another time.
My birth was here.
Swaddled in linens of your own design.
You spun the threads beside the fire
on the cold December nights.

What is this now
my Other?
Frozen glare you call your Muse
I call our original sin.

Keyholes

Closer
  is the breath
  pirouettes
  waves of the winds

Speaks
  in silhouettes
  of 2 figures
  searching sand
  for sun-warmth

Touching
  each intimate corner
  of the dark chests
  thru the minute keyholes
  without disturbing
  one
  single
  web.

To The Keeper Of The Books

I find in your soft face
that transient lover
so common an occurrence
to my dreams.

That stature
                    muscle texture
                              great, kind hands
hands which must have known more
than all these books.

Books to the ceilings, piles on the floors
yet kept in perfect order
as if the importance were deeply known.

Will you ever come to know me
half as well?

No matter . . .

I find in your soft face
caring in the late afternoons
over red wine and talk of Russian novelists
like warm rummed milk in Siberian nights

These times gentle me thru dusk
reassure me of dawn.

The Genius

Houses can not contain
your vast uncertainties.
Stairs have feared your stepping,
tables whisper your name.
Even the walls know your thoughts.
Racking the brain, searching
in quest of new answers.
Certain that they will lead you
around to a finer
Life . . . one with more meanings.

Forgetting each past day
unsure of the next.
Giving in to the madness
until winds shift the tides.
Endings know their places.

Sinking

She stares, wide eyed into spaces
that are not our own.

Dances, snapping long fingers to songs
which are not in our pitch.

It is said that her mother died
holding this child from the water.

This child now walks, head raised
to aid the task.

This child has bruises on her arms
twenty years to date from this event.

This child stares, sinking to where
the sun can not reach.

Sinking down, past her father's
outstretched hands.

Sinking down, to the place
where there are no sounds.

I want to go with her.

Staying Too Long

She
has
knelt
on soft pine

to regard
the orange
mushrooms
which light
the darkness
with a radiance
like sun
never
come to warm
this place

completing her joy
she stands

but her legs
are numb
her feet ache
her eyes will not
close

She has always
feared this.

That
the world
is a dark floor
where mushrooms
grow
and once they
lay claim to you
declare their plot
of loam

you can never
return to
sun.

Dragon

Like some conquered dragon
heart of white gold
but the scales give you away
that and your infernal breathing.

you lie quiet in your cave
hunger has made you lucid
images dance on the walls
lightened by your breathing.

Was it your own teeth
which inflicted such a wound?
you feel the point of entry
exit
with every breath
wonder if it is enough
to kill you

it is.

Moorings

This wind comes softly to surround us.
Hands, together, barely touching.
Fingering the motions of our air.

This must be another time and space
where the pages of my poems
are passed out like communion wafers
sit on your tongue
                                        you let them dissolve
let me watch
empty tongued you spoke of leaves
how your image may come to sit
on one of mine.

Were you hoping to hold back autumn?
Wishing it may end this continence?

Your ship is moored tightly
and I have little faith that I may loosen it
only slight desire to try
for within this wind, coming softly to surround us
lays that gentlest of man with woman eyes
who knows perverse desires of gulls
with broken wings.

On Being Single

How do they get here?
What do they want?
These proud men who walk
beside the deep black ground.
Strutting, kicking down
the myrtle groves
as they pass death

Coming closer
closer
I can count their days
on one slender hand
ask only for their
pace to quicken.

Slowly they sift
through my narrowness
and the sand pyramid
grows each time
only to be turned
again
and again.

Why do they come here?
What do they want?
When do they feel time
like fallen leaves
like hands
letting go
from trying to
nestle closer
cuddle the lilacs
like immortality
study each nitch
of my silent palm
as if it were
something rare
or fine
or carved by God.

How do they get here?
What do they need?

For Hellman, Capote & All The Rest

In New Orleans
everyone eventually dies
and gets put
in above ground
stone tombs.

This is because
below ground
all the world is damp
and bayou black.

Walking these graveyards
is like walking
through God's mouth.

When the wind blows
off the warm waters
God sings all his children
to sleep.

First one, then the next,
then the next
until the unison sound
of all the sleeping dead
wakes up the living
who must get up
and write it down.

The White Cottage

(and the Egyptian landlord)

When I came here
to this tall place
you knew that these
small rooms
could contain me,
yet let me stretch
my nouns, but most
of all
my adjectives.

You are brown skinned
and show the history
of your essence
much more ancient
than my own.
Was it that rich
knowing or just
intuition that
you knew my first
born self could
breathe life
within these walls?

You would not let me
cover up the bone-beams
but made me live with
my history
listen to the night tales
until I knew them
by heart.

How I envy you
and the depth
of your history
touching sand
touching stone.
We do share a
common reverence
for hieroglyphics
though mine are
all my poems.

In the darkness
when the tree frogs
perform their cacophony
of visual sound
I almost hear you
listening for my pen
crossing paper
awaiting birth
to make this house
whole.

P.L.F.

(Parachute Landing Fall)
for the woman at Lakewood who never pulled the cord

the air, it breathed a perfect sigh
inviting her to touch, be touched
by the world of void
the sight of the total thing

she had come to know it well
to trust implicitly, the air
far more than land or water

& the tiny plane kept up it's climb
past the flock of Canadas
past the horse tail clouds
until the sails of the boats
lost all their colors & everything
was blue

the noise, always deafening
the thrill, always that dry mouth
palpatating, almost perfect pain

pushing past the strength of air
she stands outside the plane
upon a 4 inch wide board
breathes deep, arches firmly
and loosens her grip on solid things

& the letting go, the falling
though never like the falling
of her dreams, but more like
floating . . .

stretching her arms & legs
to buy more time until
this one time
god reaches down, holds her
suspended, as if forever
in midair

finally he has found her
& she licks the manna from his
fingertips & she smells
the scent of his forgiveness
comes to the knowing of
his timelessness

never seeing how swiftly the earth
approaches
never realizing that life's dome
has been kept bundled close to her body

never caring when she reaches the ground
& the earth welcomes her like a stone

& everything gets broken
save her unity.

Healing

I
want to be
where the sun warms my orange pillows

I
want to be
where the towhees invite me to tea

I
want to be
where the channel bell becomes my heartbeat

I
want to be
where the people I meet are in the novels I read

I
want to be
where everything is in whites and in blues

I
want to be
on the island where the world can not find me
and only the pine trees remember my name

Dust & Resurrection

We all lived in and around a grey concrete pool. Our area was small, and while we swam, we could see a grey concrete building in the distance with beams of light emerging from it which played in the tall grasses. To the right were tall cliffs with five arched openings halfway up the cliff. To the left was a forest consisting of tall trees and a imperturbable tangle of vines. We ate only what was in the pool. Mostly small crawfish, large grey fish, and various types of black insects. Some of us had tried to hunt on land, but had little success.

On this particular day, there were about 20 of us in the pool. I knew only a few of them, and the strangers would not speak with me. It became evident that an older man at the end of the pool had it in his mind to get me killed that day. He intimidated me enough to send me after the largest fish in the pool. Just as I was about to grasp the fish, the man threw a spear, missing me by only a fraction of an inch, but hitting the fish with a nauseating thud. I was temporarily blinded by the profusion of fish blood which turned my face and hair red. I was terrified of this man, but knew that I was somehow protected from him. My protectors name was Nimrod. He seemed to understand much more than I could ever hope to.

We all thought that all reality was contained here, within the small limits of our sight. The others were satisfied with this, but I wanted to know what was in the arched caves. Others told me that the caves were the eyes of the gods which watched us constantly. Nimrod only smiled and told me that perhaps I should go and explore the caves, confiding in me that he had once gone when he was my age.

That night I was transported to the caves on a beam of light. The ground of the cave was covered with a layer of fine dust, and I was in the center, looking out at the stars through the arches. Five beams of white light converged on me and I could see the scene from two points of view. It was as if I was watching myself from above, and I could also see through my own eyes to the outer limits of the cave. The wind blowing through the arches, never disturbed the dust, but it's sound made me want to dance.

I bowed my head and raised my arms watching with wonder how every step which I took left an indelible impression in the dust. I was a small Greek boy dressed in a white tunic and I was dancing to the sounds of the wind and the light. God then spoke to me, without using words. He spoke to me in my head. He said that I was being tested. He was looking for his Adam, and I was being tested to see if I would do. He told me that the world had been created for me, and I was the only reality. I asked him to send me back to Ephesus, but he showed me the letters written on the wall. Although I couldn't read, I knew that the letters had the message "The Aegean must be saved."

I then stood in the last archway and watched as he changed the grey building into a hundred fountains which came alive in the light which he had shown on them. He told me to sleep now for tomorrow I must tell him the five most hated things on earth. I slept uneasily wondering if I should tell God about the old man and the spear.

When I awoke, I was back at the pool, and Nimrod was massaging my brow with herbs. He looked at me, eye to eye, and asked if I now understood that this was all created for me. I was afraid. Now Nimrod too might be unreal. He took my hand and lead me into the water. My enemy instantly approached me and told me that my breakfast was at the end of the pool, waiting for me. It was an enormous fish, and when I dove in to capture it with my bear hands, it turned into a capsule which sprouted milk. I was so confused, all that I could think of was that if this was an enclosure which we were in, then there must be a way to get outside of it. Get away from these hateful men and their giant fishes.

I thought again about being Adam. If this was true, then I would have to go on land and learn to hunt. Here we all were, captives in a setting that was all part of God's game, and the rules were changing so rapidly that we would never have a chance to learn them. I sat beside the pool, covered with milk, crying for my beloved Ephesus.

Collecting my dreams, I hide them
in all the pockets of my skin.

I am keeping the one of loving you
hidden in the deepest pocket.

Afraid that you'd steal it
if you ever believed it.

This book was produced with the generous help of the people listed below. I would like to thank everyone who contributed money, time, energy and emotional support in the creation of "Hysterical Fugue."

Jackie & Gordon Albert
Jeanine Babcock
Anne P. Berg
Ann & Jack Berg
Edith Berg
Susan Bingham
Anne & Nicholas Borrell
Charles M. Bowes
Marilyn & Robert Callander
Pamela Callander
David Dalton
Ed & Sue Douglas
Cynthia Fetterholf
Dan Fox
Jenny Garelli
Burt & Ilka Giges
William Golub
Constance Hamilton
Paul & Opal Horvat
Just Books
Bill Kopp
Greg Kosakow
Ann E. Kronen
Trudy Zweig Livingstone
William Lovell
Mary Lucas
Margaret Malven
Louis A. Maresca
Howard & Sidney Mihls
Cy & Peggy Nathan
Thomas J. Nathan
Linda Lowrey Newsom
Penny & Andrew
Rex Peters
Trish & Bob Pfeiffer
Michael Pullano
Percival R. Roberts
Al Rosenman
Susan Royce
Gil Sanchez & Friends
John Schreiner
Gloria Schwartz
Jill & Gary Schwilst
Joseph Sherman
Ed Snider
Pamela Stewart
Blair St. James
Helen Sullivan
Patricia Sussen
Jan-Piet Van der Horst
Carolyn & Jeff Vreeland
Joy & Bob Wassel
Jed Waterbury
Heidi Wetzel